Tuesday
December 31st 2019
2:30 P.M.

Byrd & Clay Wedding 2019

WELCOME
to the
LOVE STORY
of

HOWARD
&
RABESHIA

Byrd & Clay Wedding 2019

Byrd & Clay Wedding 2019

Once Upon A Time...

Byrd & Clay Wedding 2019

...far far away...

Two future friends were born...

Byrd & Clay Wedding 2019

Byrd & Clay Wedding 2019

Their teenage years were filled with hope and friends that loved them.

Byrd & Clay Wedding 2019

They left home to pursue their dreams and find happiness, but they realized something was missing...

Byrd & Clay Wedding 2019

Byrd & Clay Wedding 2019

However, they were unsure of what it was.

Byrd & Clay Wedding 2019

Until one day,

they both decided

to give love

one...last...try.

Byrd & Clay Wedding 2019

Byrd & Clay Wedding 2019

And then...

all the stars aligned in

their favor and

they met for the first time.

Byrd & Clay Wedding 2019

Byrd & Clay Wedding 2019

It was magic from

the very start!

They had found

what was missing…

Byrd & Clay Wedding 2019

LOVE!

Byrd & Clay Wedding 2019

Byrd & Clay Wedding 2019

LOVE grew deeper

and SMILES grew brighter...

They knew they

could never be apart.

Byrd & Clay Wedding 2019

Byrd & Clay Wedding 2019

So they made it official and shared their love with the world.

Byrd & Clay Wedding 2019

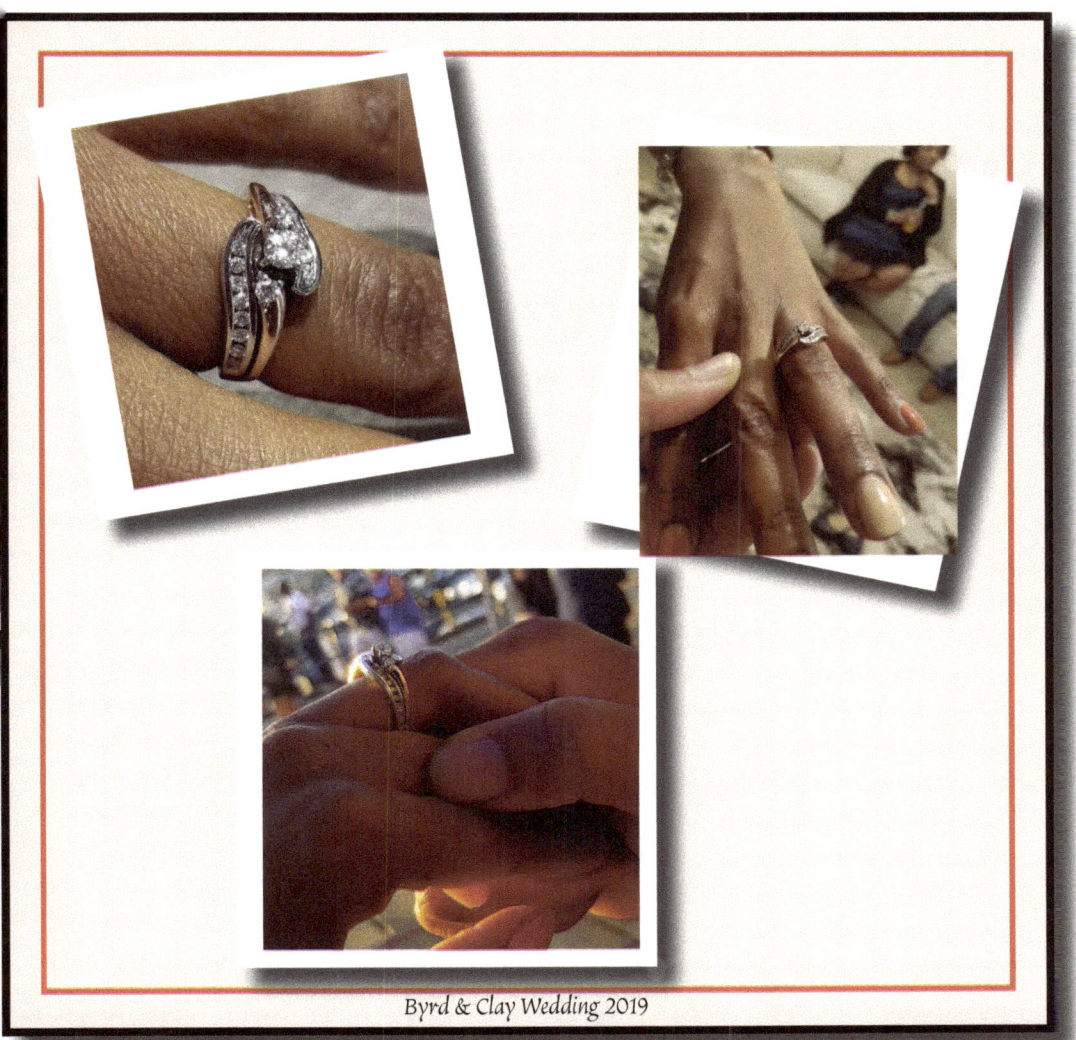

Byrd & Clay Wedding 2019

It wasn't long

before they set a date…

and invited their

friends and family.

Byrd & Clay Wedding 2019

Byrd & Clay Wedding 2019

So, today…

YOU have become a

part of OUR

love story!

Byrd & Clay Wedding 2019

Byrd & Clay Wedding 2019

2020

is filled with promises

and new beginnings.

Thank you for being here to

share this moment with us.

Byrd & Clay Wedding 2019

The End.
(Which is really just the beginning!)

Special Thanks:

Ralph and Bessie Byrd
Linda and Howard Clay Sr.
Crystal Byrd
Carrie DuBose
D'vante Black
Jeff Clay Jr
Valhalla McGauhey
Laura Aceituno
Uncle Charlie and Aunt Monica

Byrd & Clay Wedding 2019

www.ingramcontent.com/pod-product-compliance
Lightning Source LLC
Chambersburg PA
CBHW061148010526
44118CB00026B/2911